THE *FANTASTIC* BOOK OF

HORSES

JANE PARKER

COPPER BEECH BOOKS
BROOKFIELD, CONNECTICUT

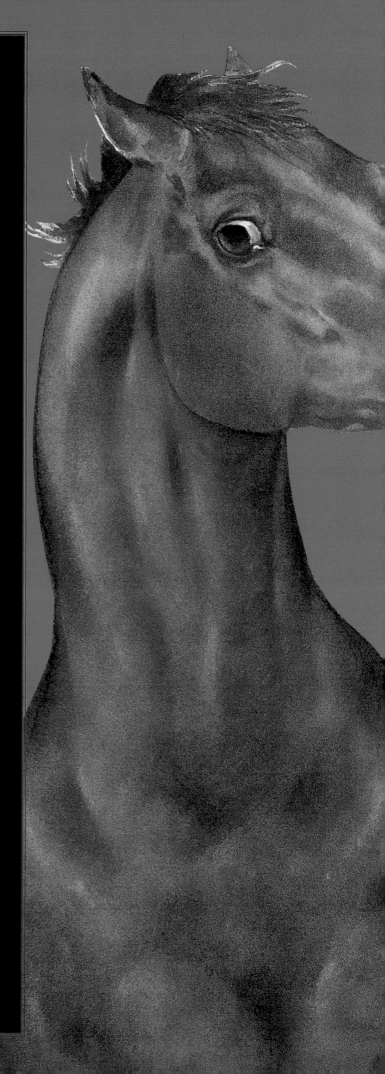

© Aladdin Books Ltd 1997

Designed and produced by
Aladdin Books Ltd
28 Percy Street
London W1P 0LD

First published in the United
States in 1997 by
Copper Beech Books,
an imprint of
The Millbrook Press
2 Old New Milford Road
Brookfield, Connecticut 06804

Editor
Sarah Levete
Design
David West
Children's Book Design
Designer
Rob Perry
Illustrator
Steve Roberts, Wildlife Art Agency
Picture Research
Brooks Krikler Research
Consultant
Elwyn Hartley Edwards

Printed in Belgium

Library of Congress
Cataloging-in-Publication Data

Parker, Jane.
Horses / by Jane Parker ; illustrated by Steve
Roberts
p. cm. -- (The fantastic book of--)
Includes index.
Summary: Discusses how horses live and
compete, how to care for them, and how they
are used.
ISBN 0-7613-0566-1 (lib. bdg.). -
- ISBN 0-7613-0580-7 (trade hc)
1. Horses--Juvenile literature.
2. Horsemanship--Juvenile literature.
[1. Horses. 2. Horsemanship.] I. Roberts,
Steve, ill. II. Title. III. Series.
SF302.H42 1997   96-48289
636.1--dc21   CIP AC

C O N T E N T S

THE FOLD-OUT SECTION

INTRODUCTION

Horses and ponies are wonderful animals with whom you can develop a long and trusting friendship. This can lead to a rewarding interest, or even profession, in adult life.

Young people often long to own their own pony or horse. But this is a huge responsibility. The animals depend on regular daily care throughout the year, and will suffer if it is missed. The best way to learn about horses is with lessons on riding and horse management from a qualified instructor at a licensed riding school. This is probably also the best place to keep a first pony, where expert advice is always available.

Whether or not you are already a rider or even an owner of a horse or pony, this book is packed with information on riding, handling, and caring for horses and ponies as well as their anatomy and different breeds.

From preparation to the winner's parade, the eight-page fold-out section takes you eventing, from a one-day event to a top-class three-day event, one of the most demanding of all equestrian sports.

Looking after a horse or pony is hard work, but when he or she demonstrates trust in you or wins a rosette for you, it is well worth it.

4

There are often white hairs
(below) *growing down a
horse's face that can be
used for identification.
The marking may
extend over the
entire face or
just be a fleck
on the
forehead.*

forelock

poll

mane

muzzle

crest

MEASURING a HORSE
*Horses are measured from the
highest point of the withers to
the ground. The unit of
measurement is a
"hand" (4 inches).*

withers

chin groove

throat

jugular groove

point of shoulder

chest

Interrupted stripe

Star

Blaze

Points of the HORSE

No one horse or pony is the same. Each has her own individual
temperament and look, from color to the patterns of the
markings. Each face marking *(see above)* is unique to the horse
or pony, just like a human "fingerprint" is to a person. A horse's
overall shape is called her conformation, and is often the result
of her breeding. When you care for and ride
horses, you need to learn the terms that are
used to identify and describe them. These
include the names of the colors, from
skewbald (white and another color) to
piebald (black and white), and the
names of the markings and the different
parts, or points, of the horse's body.

foreleg

knee

cannon bone

ergot

hoof

*The picture
shows the most important points
of the horse. You may know a
few – but try and learn them all!*

6

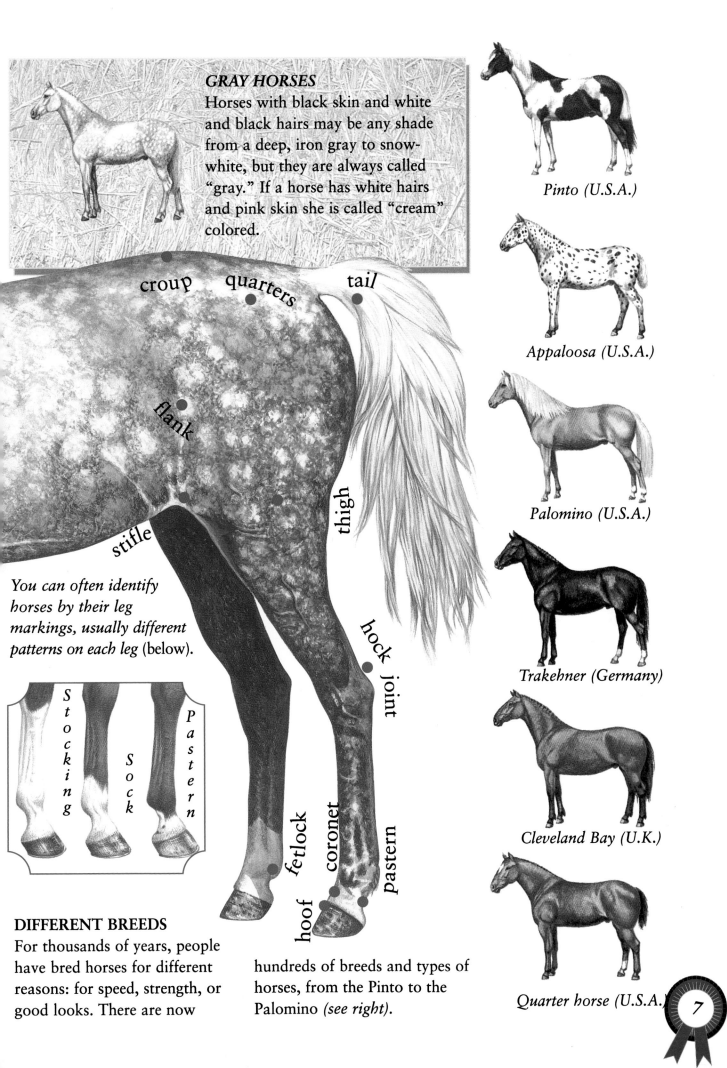

GRAY HORSES
Horses with black skin and white and black hairs may be any shade from a deep, iron gray to snow-white, but they are always called "gray." If a horse has white hairs and pink skin she is called "cream" colored.

croup   quarters   tail

flank

thigh

stifle

You can often identify horses by their leg markings, usually different patterns on each leg (below).

hock joint

Stocking   Sock   Pastern

fetlock   coronet

hoof   pastern

DIFFERENT BREEDS
For thousands of years, people have bred horses for different reasons: for speed, strength, or good looks. There are now hundreds of breeds and types of horses, from the Pinto to the Palomino *(see right)*.

Pinto (U.S.A.)

Appaloosa (U.S.A.)

Palomino (U.S.A.)

Trakehner (Germany)

Cleveland Bay (U.K.)

Quarter horse (U.S.A.)

MUSCLES
Attached to bones by tendons at each end, muscles work in pairs contracting and relaxing to make the bones move. The horse's "engine," which propels him forward, lies in the muscles in the hindquarters.

skull

jawbone

Anatomy of A HORSE

To help you learn how best to ride and care for your horse or pony, it is important that you understand how his bones are put together and how the muscles work. Horses are mammals just like dogs and cats, but they run on the tips of their toes and have hooves instead of claws. The bodies of their wild ancestors were designed for speed, so they could escape from predators. Today, horses often have to bear considerable weight or perform athletic or complex movements as the Lipizzaner horse *(above)* does. Whatever your horse does, bring him to fitness by gradual training. Always gently warm him up before he starts hard work.

scapula

elbow joint

humerus

radius

HORSES and PONIES
A "horse" is usually more than 14.2 h or 57 inches (see page 6) and a "pony" is under that height. However, these terms can refer to body proportions. A pony is deeper in the body and shorter legged in relation to its height than a horse. A stocky Shetland pony (far left) is about 40 inches while the Falabella horse (left) only reaches 30 inches.

HOW TO TELL A HORSE'S AGE

By six years old, horses have lost their first (milk) teeth, and their permanent teeth are in place. Their teeth grow all the time, wearing away as they grind their food. You can tell a horse's age – they can live up to 40 years old – by looking at the shape and condition of his teeth *(left)*.

spine

ileum

femur

ribs

tibia

cannon

HORSE EVOLUTION

The first ancestor of the horse, the *Hyracotherium*, was a small animal with toes. Adapting to different climates and conditions over millions of years resulted in the evolution of animals such as Przewalski's wild horse *(above)*. The modern horse *(below)* is the result of breeding by people rather than natural evolution.

BONES

Like a human, a horse's body is supported on a framework of bones known as the skeleton. Where two bones meet, a joint is formed. The ends of the bones are smooth and are held together by strong ligaments that allow a certain amount of movement.

MARE, STALLION, AND FOAL

An adult female horse is called a mare. An adult male is called a stallion. If he has had an operation to prevent him from fathering, or siring, offspring, he is known as a gelding. Young horses up to one year old are known as foals: Female foals are fillies and males are colts.

Mare and foal

SLEEPING ON HIS FEET

A horse sleeps for about four hours a day, dozing for short periods. If he feels safe, he will sleep lying down.

If he senses possible danger, he will sleep standing up – his elbow and stifle joints and ligaments "lock" to stop him falling over while dozing.

9

Horse SENSE

Horses are sociable animals. In groups, one horse will become the leader; some will form friendships, while others may become bullies. Horses communicate their moods and intentions to each other by using body postures and facial expressions. Sounds and smells are also important. Be aware of what the differences in facial expressions mean; look at your horse's eyes, ears, and nostrils, so that you can interpret her body language. Take time to get to know your horse so that you establish a safe and trusting relationship.

FEAR
This horse is alert to something he doesn't understand – he is ready to take flight with his ears back, nostrils flared, and mouth tight.

ATTENTION
This horse has seen something that has interested her: Her ears are pricked forward in the same direction.

CONTENTMENT
This horse is happy. His face is relaxed, his ears are neither pricked nor back. His eyes are dreamy, and his top lip is long.

FEELING AT EASE

Make your horse or pony aware of your presence by talking quietly to her as you approach and while you move around. A horse can grow uneasy when she senses something behind her. A gentle hand on your horse *(above)* will reassure her. To soothe a restless horse, scratch the side of her withers or between her front legs – she may try to scratch you back, just as she would another horse! Horses enjoy nuzzling each other while in the field – they like to be gently patted by humans.

WARNING
Never walk or stand behind a horse or pony you don't know. Sudden movements or noises can alarm them – you can get hurt.

SENSE OF SMELL

When in full gallop, a horse fully opens her nostrils *(right)*. Horses have an acute sense of smell. When a horse smells something unusual, she raises her head and curls back her upper lip. This is known as "flehmen."

THREAT
This horse is warning that she may attack. With flared nostrils and ears back, she opens her mouth to bite as she lunges forward. The whites of a horse's eyes often show when she rolls them as she attempts to locate the source of her alarm.

ANNOYANCE
With his ears half back, his mouth tightened, and his nose wrinkled, this horse is signaling his irritation. A wrinkled nose can also mean that the horse is in pain.

SLEEPY
With head lowered, eyes half shut, and ears drooping, this horse feels safe enough to let her guard down as she drifts off to sleep.

Living indoors, LIVING OUTDOORS

Stabling protects finer horse breeds from cold, wet weather. Keeping horses in a stable also means that they stay clean and are close at hand, ready for work. Their food intake can also be strictly tailored to their needs. You must give stabled horses the freedom to relax daily in a safe paddock, ideally with other horses. If the winter coat has been clipped, they will need the protection of a waterproof rug. Ponies and hardier breeds of horse, providing they are not clipped, can live out in a field all year, but they should be provided with shelters.

STABLES

A stabled horse needs enough room to turn around freely and to lie down and roll without becoming trapped against the wall. The stable should be draft-free, but well ventilated and well drained.

FIELD LIFE

To prevent your pony or horse from escaping, make sure that the field is safely fenced with posts and rails, or thick hedges. A field shelter gives protection from cold winds or a hot sun. There should be a supply of clean, fresh water. Your horse or pony must be checked daily, his feet picked out, and his droppings removed from the grass to prevent the spread of worms. In winter, he will need extra food.

RUGS

To regulate body temperature, a sweat rug stops a hot horse from cooling too quickly; a New Zealand rug keeps him warm and dry outside; a stable rug *(right)* keeps him warm in a stable.

FEEDS

Grass, a horse's natural diet, is not enough to keep a working horse healthy. He needs a balance of hard and bulk feed. Hard feed (oats ⑥, different types of corn ⑧, ⑨, linseed ②, and barley grains ⑦) or a mix of these, such as horse cubes, provides energy and protein to build muscle. Bulk feed (bran ④, hay ③, sugar beet ⑤,) provides fiber to maintain the digestive system. Extras, such as carrots ①, may be added.

POISONOUS FOODS

You need to be aware of the poisonous plants that can cause illness or even death. These include acorns *(above)*, bracken, Deadly Nightshade *(below right)*, and yew. Ragwort, a yellow daisylike flower that grows in pastures, is extremely dangerous: It can cause fatal liver damage in horses.

MUCKING OUT

To ensure the health and comfort of your horse or pony, the stable must be mucked out daily *(left)*. Begin by removing the droppings and soiled straw. Lift the bedding, sweep, and air the floor. The straw needs to be replaced and replenished with fresh material, which should be banked up the sides. Some types of bedding, such as wood shavings, may only require regular picking out (the removal of droppings).

Horse TACK

For the comfort and safety of you and your horse, you should know why different pieces of tack are used and how to fit them correctly. Tack refers to riding equipment, from saddles, stirrups, and girths to bridles, bits, and reins. It includes a range of halters, saddle pads and numnahs (a pad put under the saddle for comfort), breaking and schooling equipment, boots, and blankets. Tack also includes the harness, the name given to driving gear. There may be several types of a particular piece of tack, such as the bridle, which reflect the range of uses to which horses are put. Traditionally, tack is made from good-quality, stitched leather; increasingly, however, more modern synthetic materials are being used that are lightweight and easier to clean.

Double bridle

Pelham bridle

BRIDLES

A bridle holds the bit in place so the rider can control the horse with the reins. It consists of a headpiece, throatlatch, browband, cheek pieces (from which the bit is suspended) noseband (of which there are several types), and reins. The snaffle bridle uses a single bit. The sophisticated double bridle (for experienced riders) uses two bits, a snaffle (bridoon), and the curb bit. A Pelham bridle uses a single bit and two reins.

HOW TO PUT ON A BRIDLE

1

Step 1: *Put the reins over the horse's head to keep her under control.*

Step 2: *Hold the bridle up in front of her face with your right hand. Support the bit in your left hand, pushing your thumb into the corner of the horse's mouth. Slip in the bit gently as she parts her teeth.*

3

Step 3: *Tuck her ears under the head piece, one at a time. Pull her forelock outside the browband.*

Step 4: *Do up the throatlatch, noseband, curb chain, and lip straps if used. Make sure the bit is fitted correctly and lies evenly in her mouth.*

2

4

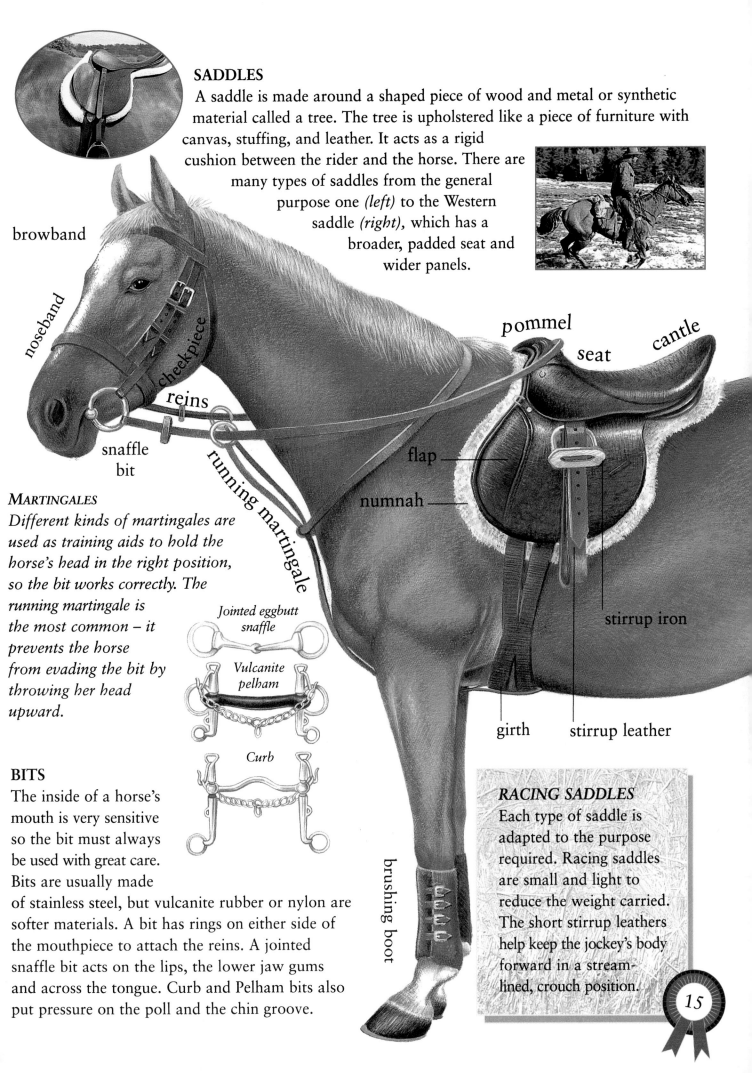

SADDLES

A saddle is made around a shaped piece of wood and metal or synthetic material called a tree. The tree is upholstered like a piece of furniture with canvas, stuffing, and leather. It acts as a rigid cushion between the rider and the horse. There are many types of saddles from the general purpose one *(left)* to the Western saddle *(right),* which has a broader, padded seat and wider panels.

browband

noseband

cheekpiece

reins

snaffle bit

running martingale

pommel

seat

cantle

flap

numnah

stirrup iron

girth

stirrup leather

brushing boot

MARTINGALES

Different kinds of martingales are used as training aids to hold the horse's head in the right position, so the bit works correctly. The running martingale is the most common – it prevents the horse from evading the bit by throwing her head upward.

Jointed eggbutt snaffle

Vulcanite pelham

Curb

BITS

The inside of a horse's mouth is very sensitive so the bit must always be used with great care. Bits are usually made of stainless steel, but vulcanite rubber or nylon are softer materials. A bit has rings on either side of the mouthpiece to attach the reins. A jointed snaffle bit acts on the lips, the lower jaw gums and across the tongue. Curb and Pelham bits also put pressure on the poll and the chin groove.

RACING SADDLES

Each type of saddle is adapted to the purpose required. Racing saddles are small and light to reduce the weight carried. The short stirrup leathers help keep the jockey's body forward in a stream-lined, crouch position.

15

Looking after TACK

It is important to clean your tack and store it neatly in the tack room. Tack is expensive and it can be uncomfortable for the horse if it is not well-maintained. Dried-up or damp leather tack may crack or even rot. In your cleaning routine, take apart the saddle or bridle. Wash off dried dirt and sweat with a warm, wet cloth. Wipe the leather dry and work in the saddle soap with a damp sponge before polishing with a dry cloth to finish off. You also need to clean and polish all the metal parts.

THE TACK ROOM
A tidy tack room has racks and hooks for saddles and bridles; tidy grooming kits; tack-cleaning materials; a bridle-cleaning hook; a saddle horse; a trunk for dry rugs and a rack for wet ones; a box for bandages and boots; and a first-aid kit.

Use leather oils and dressings to feed and soften the leather.

Use saddle soap that contains glycerine, a natural substance made from animal fats that will keep the leather supple.

Cleaning tack (right) is a routine task at the end of each day. As you clean, check the tack for wear and tear. The stitching used to join leather may rot and break, as it has on the seat of this saddle. Take any damaged tack to a tack shop for repair.

16

LOOKING AFTER SADDLES
Check your saddle regularly. The panels may need reflocking, or stuffing, to keep the tree off the horse's back. Make sure the tree is not broken – the saddle will "fold." And don't forget to check regularly that the saddle still fits your horse – his shape will change according to the work he does.

3-Day Event

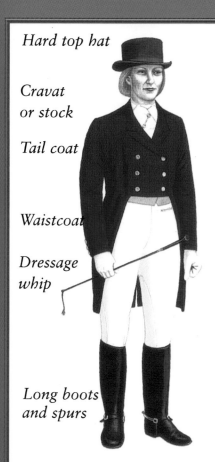

Hard top hat

Cravat
or stock

Tail coat

Waistcoat

Dressage
whip

Long boots
and spurs

*The dressage whip is for use
only while warming up.*

DAY ONE: DRESSAGE

A three-day event opens with the dressage, which is designed to show the judges that the rider is skilled and that the horse is well-trained and obedient. The actual test only lasts for about seven and a half minutes. During this time, the horse must perform, at the rider's command, a set sequence of movements at walk, trot, and canter, in front of the judges.

Walk   Trot   Canter

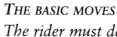

WHAT TO WEAR

The appearance of horse and rider are important in any dressage event. The rider's formal attire adds to the image of elegance, confidence, and harmony.

THE BASIC MOVES

The rider must demonstrate skill and control at walk, trot, and canter. Movements include circles and serpentines, half passes and effortless transitions (see page 28), and changes of legs. Each gait must be performed at collected, working, medium, and extended paces.

MAKING A MARK

The dressage test is held in a sanded arena, 195 feet x 65 feet. Letter markers *(right)* are placed around the arena for guidance. Each movement is performed between these set markers and is marked out of 10 by the judges seated at one end.

```
        A
F               K
P               V
B               E
D L X I G C     S
R
M               H
```

Preparing & Packing

Equipment for grooming, braiding, washing, feeding, watering, mucking out, tack, rugs, boots, bandages, first-aid kits (horse and human), and spares for everything – all this needs to be packed to take to the event with the horse, as well as the rider's outfits. At a three-day event, the rider, horse, and groom usually arrive a few days early to settle in.

a keen jumper

Each rider is registered, given a number, and a map of the course, which he or she will then walk.

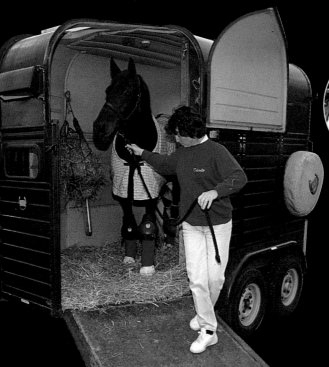

The ends of the braids are sewn with braiding thread.

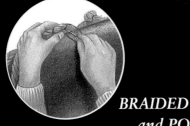

taking notice

top speed

Each braid is looped over and its end sewn to its base.

successful partnership

BRAIDED and POLISHED

The groom is responsible for the horse's appearance. Early in the morning before the dressage phase, the horse is groomed thoroughly and her mane and tail braided. Lastly, her hooves are oiled.

DRESSED for the ROAD

Whatever the distance to an event of any level, the horse should be properly dressed with a blanket for warmth, and bandages, and traveling boots to protect her legs from bumps.

The hair from underneath the tail is braided on top and the end looped over.

Eventing

A CHALLENGING TEST
Originally designed to test the horses of continental cavalry officers for obedience, endurance, and speed, eventing, today, is a demanding sport for horse and rider. Eventing tests the ability of horse and rider in dressage, cross-country, and show jumping.

QUALIFYING
Horses must compete in "prenovice" events *(above and left)*, in order to accumulate enough points to qualify for participation in a novice one-day event. They then progress through events of varying difficulty before they can compete in the most strenuous top-level three-day event.

PULLING and TRIMMING
As well as being physically fit, the horse must be perfectly turned out for the event. The longest hairs are pulled out of the mane with a comb, a few at time (below). This does not hurt the horse and leaves the mane fine enough to be easily braided.

CLIPPING and STRAPPING
Any long hairs on the fetlocks (called feathers) are clipped away with scissors and a comb (above), to make the horse's legs look more refined. Horses in training are strapped (see page 26) every day to build up muscle tone.

DAY TWO: SPEED *and* ENDURANCE

There are four phases to this exciting speed and endurance test, the most physically demanding of the competition. Phase A is road and tracks, a timed hack through country lanes and woods; phase B is the steeplechase, completed at speed along a course of about 2 miles with between 8-10 jumps; phase C is more road and tracks. Phase D, the cross-country phase, takes place after a pause for veterinary checks. Each phase must be completed within a set time.

Safety helmet with silk and body protector

SOLID FENCES
The cross-country fences are big and solid. They are designed to frighten all but the bravest horses and most determined riders.

WHAT TO WEAR: THE RIDER
Horses often fall during this demanding test, so the emphasis is on protection rather than on appearance. Riders wear crash helmets, often with silk covers in their sponsor's colors. Body protectors, worn underneath sweaters, will prevent damage to backs and ribs. White breeches, black boots, and string gloves are also usually worn.

DIFFICULT TAKEOFFS
Another formidable fence in phase D is the bank (below). Jumping over fences on uneven ground tests balance and recovery.

DIFFICULT LANDINGS
Some fences may not look very high, but there is a hidden long drop on the landing side.

Where to Stay

HOME *away from* **HOME**
Some competitors have large trucks with comfortable living quarters for both horses and humans. Others have small trailers (right) for traveling.

Eventing at the top level is very expensive – most competitors have sponsors to help them pay for the keep of the horses, all the tack, equipment, travel, and accommodation costs. If the owners do not have large trucks, the horses will stay in a rented, temporary stable erected on the trial grounds by the organizers, and the riders and grooms will stay in hotels.

WARMING *up*

Before the first event of the day, at either a one-day event (right) or a three-day event, competitors take their horses out for a short hack to "open the pipes" (stimulate breathing and circulation). The horses wear boots and bandages to protect their legs and an exercise sheet to keep them warm if the early morning air is cool.

fitness and stamina

strength

intelligence

obedience

Horses entering competitions need the attributes shown (above left).

DAY THREE: SHOW JUMPING

The final day of the three-day event begins with a thorough veterinary check of all the horses. Only those that pass this check will be allowed to finish the competition. The show jumping is designed to find out if the horse is still obedient, fit and supple after the previous two days. The rider has to walk the course, memorizing the route, counting the strides between each fence, and judging the best approach to take. The fences may be very high, or very wide, to stretch each horse to his limits. The jumping order begins with the lowest-placed competitors and finishes with the leaders.

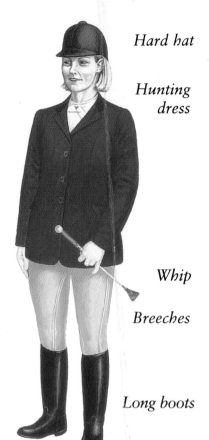

Hard hat

Hunting dress

Whip

Breeches

Long boots

The short whip is only used if the horse hesitates.

A staircase type of fence (above) encourages the horse to jump.

The top pole of the pyramid (above) is easy to rattle if the horse drops a hoof on it.

The horse must jump high and wide to clear the parallel poles on this fence (above).

Show jumping fences are often brightly colored. The poles are easily knocked off, if the horse fails to lift his legs.

WHAT TO WEAR: THE RIDER
The eventer's dress is not judged for the show jumping but most competitors wear white shirts with white stocks or ties, yellow or white breeches, and black or blue show jackets. Red hunting jackets (more correctly called "pink") are very popular and military personnel usually wear their uniforms. After the last competitor has jumped and the winner is known, all the riders assemble in the show jumping ring for a final grand parade and the prize-giving.

WHAT TO WEAR: THE HORSE

To protect the horse's legs, brushing boots *(left)* and over-reach boots prevent him from kicking himself. Studs in the shoes stop him from slipping. Most event horses wear a breastplate, a girth, and an elastic surcingle to keep the saddle in place. Grease on the front of the legs helps the horse to slide over a jump without grazing himself.

Brushing boot wraps around leg

COMING TO GRIEF

If the horse and rider fall at a fence, penalty points are added to the score (the rider with the least penalty points wins the competition). Horse and rider often get up and carry on after a fall like this (above). If the horse refuses a third time, takes the wrong route, jumps in the wrong order, or exceeds the time limit, he will be eliminated.

Care of your Horse

Eventing is very strenuous and horses can get badly hurt if they are not at the peak of their fitness. The first rule of caring for an event horse is to make sure she is fit and in perfect health. She must be on a diet that is suitable for the work she does. Horses, like athletes, should always warm up slowly before competing, or before hard work, to avoid straining muscles and joints. Afterward, if they are wet with sweat, they must be walked until they are cool and dry *(right)* and not allowed to stand around getting cold. After an event, the horse deserves a few days of rest and relaxation.

COOLING OFF PERIOD
A hot and excited horse should be sponged with tepid water to cool her down.

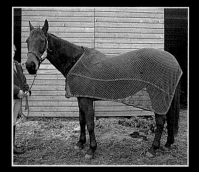

The water is removed with a sweat scraper. A sweat rug can be put on to keep her warm (above) *while she is walked around.*

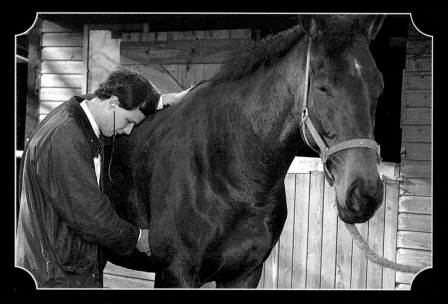

IMPRESSING *the* VET
All the horses have to pass health checks after the cross-country and before they are allowed to jump. The veterinarian examines the pulse, breathing *(above)*, and temperature of each horse and watches for any signs of lameness.

GOOD *to be* HOME
Once back in her own loose box, the tired horse will be given a small feed *(right)* and left to relax. Over the next few days, her exercise and hard feed will gradually be reduced – sudden changes in diet or the amount of exercise can do a lot of harm.

Farrier's WORK

A horse's foot is encased in a shell of horn called the hoof. Like a fingernail, the hoof grows constantly, about 0.5 inches per month. If a horse is not working, this growth must be cut away by a farrier to stop the hoof from becoming overgrown and deformed. If a horse is working, unshod, on hard surfaces, this growth can be worn away, causing soreness and lameness. Iron shoes are fitted by the farrier to protect the hoof. Farriers also carry out shoeing to treat foot problems.

Nails

The farrier's tool kit includes: a claw hammer; a rasp; a buffer; a drawing knife; hoof testers and cutters; clenching tongs; nails; pincers; a pritchel.

Clenching tongs

Rasp

Heel

Bar
Sole

Shoe

HORSES' HOOVES
The hoof horn is a tough material, divided from the sensitive tissue by a barrier called the white line. The shoe is nailed outside this line, where there is no feeling. The soft frog helps to absorb shock as the hoof strikes the ground. The bones and tissues inside the hoof are very sensitive; any injury or disease can cause severe pain. Call a veterinarian if there is any sign of lameness.

A SHOD HOOF
A well-fitting shoe fits neatly around the rim of the hoof wall, neither too long nor too short, with the clip in the center of the foot. Normally, there are four nails on the outside and three on the inside of each shoe. The shoe must be made to fit the hoof – the hoof should never be shaped to fit the shoe.

SHOEING
Step 1: Supporting the hoof between his knees, the farrier files off the clenches (the ends of the nails). He pulls off the old shoe with pincers. Then he trims away the excess horn from the sole of the hoof with cutters or a drawing knife (*above*).

Step 2: He rasps the sole until the horse stands level. He heats the new shoe to red-hot and shapes it to fit the hoof by hammering it over an anvil (*above*).

Step 3: Then he checks the fit by pressing the shoe onto the foot with a pritchel (*above*). He cools the shoe and nails it to the hoof.

25

Learning to GROOM

It is important to learn how to correctly groom your horse or pony, whether he is field-kept or stabled. Grooming is not just about making your horse look good. As you remove dirt, grease, and sweat from the horse's coat you may also be removing parasites and stimulating blood circulation to the skin. When you groom, look for signs of injury or illness. And don't forget – your horse probably enjoys being groomed and he will get to know you better as you move around him.

GROOMING TECHNIQUE

Brush the coat with a body brush in the direction that the hair lies, from the neck toward the tail and down the legs. Scrape the curry comb (below) across the brush *to remove the dirt. Brush tangles from the mane and tail a lock at a time.*

A GROOM'S DAY

"First thing, I inspect my horse, feed him, and change his covers. Then it's mucking out. I brush him and tack him up. After exercise I clean him. I'll cover him up and feed him again. I may turn him out to grass while I clean tack, tidy the yard, and prepare feeds and bedding. I'll bring him in for his evening feed and hayrack. Before bed, I water, feed, and hay him, change his covers, and pick out the stall for the last time."

Keep a stabled horse clean with a body brush. After exercising him, you can strap him (vigorously rub) with a straw wisp or pad to tone the muscles and stimulate blood circulation.

GROOMING KIT

Grooming kits should be kept clean and tidy. Dirt and hair can be removed from brushes with a metal curry comb. Everything should be regularly soaked in disinfectant and dried thoroughly. It is a good idea to have a separate kit for each horse to prevent the spread of skin infections and parasites.

Hoof pick with brush

Sponge

Body brush

GROOMING: THE FIELD-KEPT HORSE

Ponies or horses living outside produce natural oils that waterproof their thick coats and keep them warm. Vigorous brushing can reduce this protection. So grooming should involve only removing caked mud with a dandy brush, checking for injuries, and picking out the feet. Clipping is rarely necessary, but a working pony or horse can be trace-clipped (clipping only parts of the coat).

SPONGING

Each eye, the muzzle, the dock (under the tail), and the sheath (in male horses) should be wiped clean, each with a different sponge. Squeeze the sponges out in clean, warm water. Try to use different colored sponges to help you remember which one you use for which part. This simple precaution will help to prevent the spread of infection.

HOOVES

Pick them out before and after every ride. If a horse has to carry his rider's weight with a stone wedged under his foot, he will soon become lame (see page 36).

Horse GAITS

Your horse or pony has four natural gaits or movements – the walk, trot, canter, and gallop. If you understand your horse's gaits, you will find it easier to ride correctly. Watch your horse or pony when she is moving – see if you can identify the sequence and movement of her legs. With training, horses can learn to collect (shorten) or extend all their gaits. The change from one gait to another is known as a "transition." Different breeds of horses have different actions (the amount of flexion in the knees). For example, the Arab *(above)* has a long-striding action.

THE WALK

When a horse walks *(above)*, her feet strike the ground in sequence: left hind (back); left fore (front); right hind; right fore, to give four distinct, regular beats – the walk is described as a four-time movement. When walking, two of the horse's feet are in contact with the ground.

THE TROT

When a horse trots *(right)*, the diagonally opposite pairs of feet strike the ground together. The left fore and right hind strike the ground together (known as the left diagonal), followed by the right fore and left hind striking the ground together (the right diagonal). This gives a two-time movement.

TROT: TWO-TIME MOVEMENT

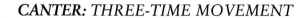

THE CANTER

The canter *(right)* is a three-time sequence that can begin on either side, depending on which way the horse is bending. On a circle to the right, for example, the sequence is: left hind; left fore and right hind together; right fore (which is the "leading" or "inside" leg in this case). A "counter-canter," when the horse leads with the outside leg, is a deliberate movement performed in a dressage test *(see page 19)* to demonstrate balance and obedience.

CANTER: THREE-TIME MOVEMENT

THE GALLOP

A full gallop *(below)* has a rhythm of four beats: left hind; right hind; left fore; right fore, followed by a moment of "full suspension" when all four feet are off the ground. As in the canter, the horse can lead with either leg but most horses have a favorite leading side. With her head and neck fully extended, and with the maximum length of her stride, the gallop is the horse's fastest gait.

ADVANCED MOVEMENTS
The classical schools of equitation, such as the Spanish Riding School in Vienna, can trace their history back hundreds of years. They teach horses to perform advanced movements or airs, such as refined kicking and rearing movements, on command. The Lipizzaner (below) *is performing an air called a "levade."*

GALLOP: FOUR-TIME MOVEMENT

$\mathcal{L}$earning to RIDE

Although it is expensive, the best and safest way to learn to ride is to have lessons from a qualified instructor. A rider tells his or her horse or pony what to do by using a system of signals called aids. The hands, the legs, the seat, and the voice are the natural aids. Artificial aids, whips, and spurs, are used to support the action of the legs. They should only be used to encourage the horse, never to punish him.

MOUNTING

Before mounting, check that the girth is secure and that the stirrup leathers are the correct length. Gather the reins, your whip, and a lock of mane in the left hand and turn to face the horse's tail. Put the left foot in the stirrup 1. Put your right hand over the waist of the saddle 2 and spring up, swinging your right leg over the saddle 3. Take care not to sit down heavily.

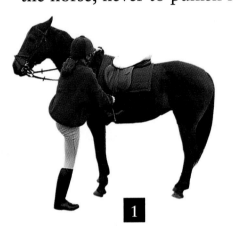

1

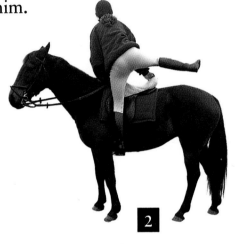

2

3

POSITION *and* WEIGHT
Balance is essential for your safety and to enable the horse to move freely. Keep your weight over the horse's center of balance. Sit upright, as if there is an imaginary straight line from your ear to your shoulder, hip, and heel (right).

HOLDING *the* REINS
Pass the rein between your last two fingers, and between your thumb and first finger. Hold your hands above the withers, thumbs on top with your wrists slightly flexed.

LEGS *and* FEET
Squeeze your legs just behind the girth to ask for forward movement and control of the horse's hindquarters. Bend your knees slightly on the saddle, with your lower legs in light contact with the horse.

Keep your toes (pointing upward and inward) in line with your knees and your heels in line with your your hips.

HAND *and* VOICE
Your hands control the bit via the reins to give instructions about speed and direction. Good riders have "light," or sensitive hands. Use your voice to give commands to your horse.

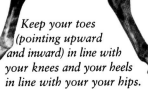

Say "up"   *Say "down"*

RISING TROT

For a beginner, the trot is a difficult gait to master. A new rider has to learn how to avoid bouncing, which is uncomfortable for both horse and rider. Listen to the beat of the trotting horse; translate the "clip-clop" into "up-down." As you say "up" push your weight up from your thighs. Sit down gently as you say "down." Never pull yourself up with the reins.

CANTERING

The canter is a more comfortable rocking motion. It is easiest to ask for canter as the horse is trotting around a bend. Sit down in your saddle; increase the rein contact slightly; and squeeze with your legs. As soon as the horse makes the transition to canter, relax the aids. Keep your body in the normal position. Push your seat down into the saddle to absorb the movement.

EXERCISES
Early lessons should include exercises to improve your position and balance, strengthen the muscles you need to use and give you confidence *(below)*. These are done first while the horse is standing with a handler holding him or leading him forward. Advanced exercises can be carried out while the horse is trotting on a lunge rein.

1

2

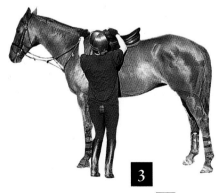

3

STOP AND DISMOUNT

To ask your horse to stop, push your weight into the saddle; apply light pressure with both legs; "feel" the horse's mouth with both reins; say "whoa." Relax the aids when he stops. Hold the reins in the left hand; take both feet out of the stirrups. Place the palm of your right hand on the saddle; lean forward ☐1. Swing your right leg back and over the cantle. Pause, leaning over the saddle ☐2 before slipping to the ground ☐3.

31

$\mathcal{L}$earning to JUMP

When you have learned how to control the horse and you feel confident with a secure and well-balanced seat, you are ready to learn how to jump. Take some lessons on an experienced horse since she will be able to measure her strides correctly as she approaches a jump. You will only have to ride her at the center of the obstacle and stay on while she goes over. You must give the horse enough freedom to use her neck, shoulders, back, and hindquarters effectively.

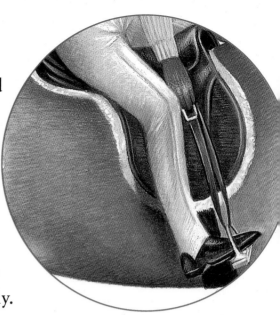

APPROACH AND TAKE-OFF
As the horse approaches the jump, she will extend her stride and lower her head. She will then bring her hindquarters

underneath her body as she prepares to take off *(above)*.

*POSITION **and** BALANCE*
You must not upset the horse's balance during any stage of the jump. Practice the correct "jumping seat" while going over ground poles (above left). Lean slightly forward with your seat out of the saddle, keeping your weight over the horse's shoulders. Look straight ahead and allow the horse to lower her head.

LUNGING LESSONS
A long lunge line and whip allows the instructor to control the horse (below). As the horse goes around in circles at a walk, trot, or canter, you can concentrate on your balance and posture.

STIRRUPS

The correct stirrup length enables you to position your legs correctly and to keep your balance. Before you begin jumping, shorten your stirrups one or two holes. This helps you to keep your weight forward while jumping. Practice altering the stirrup leathers from the saddle (left). At first, you may have to look down at the buckle.

THE NEXT JUMP

Your horse will not know in which order obstacles are to be jumped. Indicate which way she should turn before she lands, so that she can change her leading leg if necessary.

FLIGHT AND LANDING

Bend your upper body close to your horse as she curves over the jump making a shape called the bascule. Allow her all the freedom she needs to clear the jump – any interference with her balance will make her drop her legs onto the jump. As she lands, straighten up – absorb the shock with your seat and hips. Your weight should now be farther back to allow your horse to lift her shoulders as she recovers herself (*below*).

SHOW JUMPING

Once you have mastered the principles of jumping, you will probably want to start competing. Show jumping is a highly competitive sport, from the leading rein pony class at the local show to the top international competitions. The picture shows Alexandre Ledermann jumping to win France's 77th medal in the 1996 Olympics Games in Atlanta.

33

Horse EVENTS

Competitive equestrian events test all the qualities of horses and ponies and the skills of their riders. There is a lot of publicity for the big international events where the very best horses and riders compete. However, competition at local shows can be just as fierce. There are jumping classes for the smallest children on leading rein ponies and elementary dressage classes, as well as qualifiers for national competitions.

THE PONY CLUB
Founded in 1929, the Pony Club has branches worldwide. Pony clubs encourage young people to have fun with ponies while promoting the best standards of riding and care. Training is provided at regular rallies.

TEKKING
Long rides in the countryside are known as treks. A trek may be for a day or for a whole vacation. Pony trekking is great fun, whether or not you are an experienced rider. The ponies are quiet and surefooted.

GYMKHANAS
Gymkhanas were originally a form of relaxation for cavalry soldiers in India. Today these mounted games are enjoyed by thousands of young people of varying abilities on ponies of all types.

OLYMPICS
Equestrian events were first featured in the Olympic Games in 1900 in Belgium. Today teams and individuals compete in show jumping, dressage as here, in Barcelona, Spain, 1992 (below).

*W*orking HORSES

Horses have served people on farms and on battlefields, for transportation and for pleasure for thousands of years. Modern horses have been bred to work, and if they are well cared for and fit, they enjoy it. However, some are not kept fit enough for the work they are expected to do and suffer as a result. There are organizations, such as the International League for the Protection of Horses that rescue and treat these unfortunate animals and try to educate their owners.

ON *the* FARM

Heavy horses took over from oxen and donkeys for plowing and harvesting in the eighteenth century. But their use dwindled when farms became mechanized and many breeds came close to extinction. However, today, these powerful animals can be seen working on many traditional "museum farms."

WORKING WITH DISABLED PEOPLE

Well-trained, quiet ponies, accompanied by volunteer helpers, are used for riding and driving for disabled people. They help provide exercise and stimulation for people with both physical and learning difficulties.

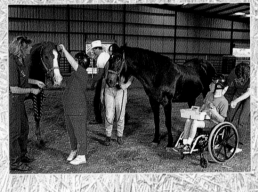

POLICE HORSES

Police forces all over the world use horses to help with crowd control. They are carefully trained to be obedient and unfazed by the loud noises they experience in busy city streets. When they are on riot patrol, they wear special protective face masks.

RANCHING

Horses are ideal for tending to animals grazing over vast areas of rough ground, whether it is sheep in the Australian outback, horses in the Carmargue in Southern France, or cattle in North and South America *(above)*. The skills of the cowboy and South American gaucho (cattle-herder) and his stock horse form the basis of rodeo eventing.

Your horse's HEALTH

A fit horse in good condition is alert with a bright, shining coat, and her skeleton is nicely covered with well-toned muscles but no fat. Health care begins with feeding. A horse on an inadequate diet will lose condition. Too much high-energy food, however, can also be dangerous. Over-fed ponies get laminitis, a very painful foot condition. It is important to know the signs of health or illness, what to look for, how to treat minor ailments and injuries, and when to call the veterinarian. If your horse is unwell, she may need "box rest," when she has to stay in her stable. If so, give her low-energy food.

LAMENESS

To identify which leg is lame, watch the horse trot. If a foreleg is lame she will nod as her good foot strikes the ground; if a hind-leg is lame she will lift the hip of the lame leg. Feel each leg for signs of pain or swelling.

SIGNS OF ILL HEALTH

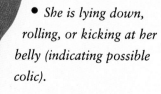

- *The horse is not as eager and interested as usual.*

- *Her resting breathing rate is above 12 times per minute (her flanks move in and out as she breathes) and it is labored or noisy.*

- *She has not drunk as usual and her urine is an unusual color.*

- *She has lost her appetite.*

- *Her mucus membranes inside her eyelids, lips, and nostrils are not bright pink.*

- *She has a discharge from her nostrils.*

- *Her coat is "staring," or standing on end.*

- *She is sweating for no reason.*

- *Her resting pulse is above or below 40 beats per minute (feel under the horse's jaw or inside the top of the foreleg).*

- *Her temperature is above 100° F (take it just inside the anus).*

- *She is lying down, rolling, or kicking at her belly (indicating possible colic).*

- *She cannot stand squarely on all four legs.*

- *She has produced abnormal droppings or no droppings.*

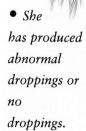

36

SECURITY

To avoid theft, install a burglar alarm on the stables and always keep tack rooms locked. Keep gates to fields and yards chained and padlocked at both ends to prevent them from being lifted from their hinges. Horses can be painlessly marked with security numbers by freeze-marking (left), hoof-branding, tattooing, or a tiny identifying radio chip that can be inserted beneath the horse's skin by a vet.

KEEPING RECORDS

Keep a health record for your horse so that you know her usual breathing rate, pulse, and temperature. Write down when wormers and vaccinations are given. You can also write down any loss of appetite or performance, or minor injuries and how they were treated, in case they develop into more serious problems.

CHECKLIST

Check daily for general health, lameness, and minor injuries. An annual veterinary check (below) includes teeth rasping and vaccinations for tetanus and influenza.

It is a good idea to keep a file or folder with important information on your horse or pony. Make a daily, weekly, monthly, and annual health care checklist. Write down the things that you need to check. Tick them off as you do them.

For example, your 5–6 weekly checklist should include:

Get hooves trimmed;
Get hooves reshod;
Give wormers to remove internal parasites.

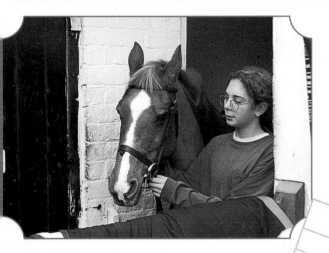

A healthy mare and her lively new foal (right).

$\mathcal{Y}$our SAFETY

Horses are large and strong, and learning how to handle and ride them correctly is the first rule of safety. When you ride, choose a safe route away from busy roads, go with a friend, and always tell someone where you are going and when you will be back. Take out a special horse-and-rider insurance policy just in case you are involved in an accident. Always wear the correct protective clothing.

GLOVES
Riding gloves (above) have leather or rubber patches between the third and fourth finger to help you grip the reins. You will need two pairs – one to look smart while riding and another to keep your hands dry and warm when you are mucking out on cold, muddy days.

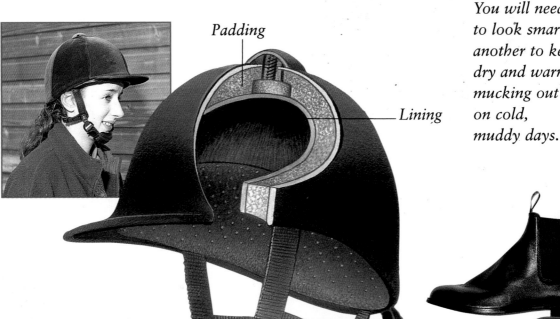

Padding

Lining

3-point harness

PROTECT YOURSELF
A fall or kick from a horse can result in serious injury. When you are around horses or when you are riding, wear a hard hat that meets the approved standard, such as a peaked, covered hat *(above)*, or a crash helmet *(right)*. Body protectors *(see page 20)* help to prevent damage to your spine.

FOOTWEAR *and* JODPHURS
For riding, wear short or long boots with a heel (above). Flat-soled shoes may slip through the stirrup iron, and buckles can get stuck. Wear jodhpurs (below) or tight-fitting pants with extra layers to protect the inside of the knees.

BE SEEN
Riders should wear fluorescent or day-glow straps or vests with added reflective strips, so that they can be seen on the roads in dim light. Horses can wear bandages and exercise sheets made of similar materials.

Horse Words

Aids
The means by which a rider communicates with his or her horse.

Airs
The movements performed by the highly trained horses of the classical schools of equitation.

Anatomy
An animal's internal structure.

Bascule
The shape made as a horse curves over a jump with his or her legs tucked up.

Breeding
A horse's ancestry which gives conformation, color, and ability.

Bridle
A set of straps worn on the horse's head to keep the bit in the correct place in the mouth.

Brushing
When a horse strikes the inside of one leg with the hoof of another, usually inside the fetlock joint.

Change of leg
When a horse changes the leading leg at the canter as he or she changes direction.

Collection
When the horse's outline is shortened and rounded as the hindlegs are brought underneath his or her body.

Conformation
The physical structure or shape of a horse.

Contact
The amount of feel on the reins linking the rider's hands to a horse's mouth.

Dressage
Exercises performed on flat ground to show the suppleness, agility, and obedience of a horse.

Equestrian
This term refers to anything to do with horses – the name is from *Equus*, the Latin for horse.

Eventing
A competition to test the horse's ability at dressage, cross country, and show jumping. Originally designed by the military to test cavalry horses.

Extension
Lengthening the stride.

Flehmen
When a horse curls back the top lip in response to a strange smell or taste – a stallion does this in the presence of a mare.

Gait
The movements (walk, trot, canter, and gallop) made naturally by a horse.

Grooming
Cleaning a horse and making him or her look tidy.

Hack
A ride out on a horse.

Lunge rein
A long rein attached to a bridle or headcollar to keep a horse going around the trainer in circles.

Martingale
A strap or straps that prevent a horse from putting his or her head up.

Numnah
A protective pad fitting between a horse and saddle.

Picking out
Removing droppings from the stable or paddock.

Points
The parts of a horse's body.

Rasping
Filing a horse's hoof.

Saddle
A seat that allows the rider to sit correctly on a horse.

Stall
A stable with a door where the horse can be left loose.

Strapping
A form of massage that helps to tone a horse's muscles. It involves vigorous strokes with a straw wisp.

Surcingle
A buckled belt that fastens around a horse's body to hold a rug, blanket, or saddle in place.

Thoroughbred
Horses bred for racing whose ancesters can be traced back to three Arab stallions in the 1700s.

Transition
The change from one gait to another.

Index

Photo Credits: *Abbreviations: t-top, m-middle, b-bottom, r-right, l-left*

4-5, 6tm, 14 all, 17 all, 18m, 23tl, tr, mb, bl & br, 24bl, 26b, 30b, 31m, 32bl & br, 36tl & 37bl – Kit Houghton; 6tl, tr & bl, 8tr, 10tr, 11tl, 12ml, 13 all, 16m, br, 20tr, 22t, 24tl, mr & br, 26t, 27 all, 30tl, tm, tr & br, 35br, 37br, 38 all – Roger Vlitos; 1, 12tl & br, 16tl, 24tr, 25 all, 28t & b, 29t, 31bl, bm, br, 34bl, 37t & m – Charles de Vere; 11m, 15tl & tr, 18br & bm, 19 t & b, 20ml, 20-21b, 28l, 33b, 34tr & m, back cover – Robert Harding Picture Library; 8m, 15tr, 18t, 21tr, 22b, 29br, 33b, 34b, 35r – Frank Spooner Pictures; 20bl – Rex Features; 11tr, 28m, 29bl, 32m, 33m, 35ml – Bruce Coleman Collection.

The publishers would like to thank the Waffrons School of Riding, Chessington, Surrey, for their help and co-operation in the preparation of this book.